FOCUS on Writing

Writing Frames Resource Pack

Writing Frames for
Introductory Book and Books 1–4

John Jackman
and Wendy Wren

Collins

Published by HarperCollins*Publishers* Ltd
77-85 Fulham Palace Road
London
W6 8JB

Browse the complete Collins catalogue at
www.collinseducational.com

© John Jackman and Wendy Wren 1998, Revised edition 2004

First published 2002 as part of *Focus on Writing Teacher's Guide*
This edition first published 2004

10 9 8 7
ISBN-13 978-0-00-718047-9
ISBN-10 0-00-718047-0

John Jackman and Wendy Wren assert the moral right to be identified as the authors of this work.

All rights reserved. No part of this publication may be reproduced, stored in a retrieval system, or transmitted in any form or by any other means, electronic, mechanical, photocopying, recording or otherwise, except for the pages marked *Focus on Writing* © John Jackman and Wendy Wren, HarperCollins*Publishers* 1998, without the prior consent, in writing, of the Publisher.

British Library Cataloguing in Publication Data
A catalogue record for this book is available from the British Library.

Editor: Mitzi Bales
Cover design: Neil Adams, Grasshopper Design
Designer: Philippa Jarvis
Cover photograph: Getty Images © Darren Gulin
Illustrations: Juliet Breese

Printed by Martins the Printers Ltd, Berwick

You might also like to visit
www.harpercollins.co.uk
The book lover's website

Contents

Introduction 3

Expected outcomes and key text level objectives
    Year 2   4
    Year 3   5
    Year 4   6
    Year 5   7
    Year 6   8

Photocopiable Writing Frames 9

Introduction

This **Writing Frames Resource Pack** provides a photocopiable writing frame for every unit in the *Focus on Writing* series. The writing frames offer a range of tools that support the writing process. These include planning sheets, charts for collecting and classifying words as well as prompts for writing in particular genres. The writing frames are designed to be employed in conjunction with the other resources in the series but can easily be adapted to suit a wide range of planning and writing activities.

The tables on pages 4–8 provide an easy reference point for teachers to look up the key objective covered by each writing frame, the expected outcome of the writing frame and the unit it accompanies to in the other *Focus on Writing* resources. More detailed guidance on how the writing frames can be employed can be found in the notes covering each unit in the *Focus on Writing* **Teacher's Guide**.

Expected outcomes and key text level objectives

Introductory Book Year 2

Writing Frame	Unit	Expected outcome	Key text level objective
1	1	Plan a story about a series of events, incorporating time-related language appropriately.	T1(11) to use language of time to structure a sequence of events, e.g. 'when I had finished…', 'suddenly…', 'after that…'
2	2	Use story structure to write a picture story about a series of events.	T1(10) to use story structure to write about own experience in same/similar form
3	2	Use story structure to write about a series of events using time-related language appropriately.	T1(11) to use language of time to structure a sequence of events, e.g. 'when I had finished…', 'suddenly…', 'after that…'
4	3	Write a poem using the structure of a familiar poem and substituting own ideas.	T1(12) to use simple poetry structures and to substitute own ideas, write new lines
5	4	Order instructions sequentially; write simple instructions in a logical order.	T1(15) to write simple instructions, e.g. getting to school, playing a game
6	5	Write simple instructions and organize them sequentially.	T1(16) to use models from reading to organise instructions sequentially, e.g. listing points in order, each point depending on the previous one, numbering
7	6	Plan a story/continuation focusing particularly on the setting.	T2(13) to use story settings from reading, e.g. re-describe, use in own writing, write a different story in the same setting
8	7	Plan simple character descriptions.	T2(14) to write character profiles, e.g. simple descriptions, posters, passports, using key words and phrases that describe or are spoken by characters in the text
9	8	Write concise definitions; organize definitions alphabetically.	T2(20) to make class dictionaries and glossaries of special interest words, giving explanations and definitions, e.g. linked to topics, delivered from stories, poems
10	9	Produce a flow chart or diagram showing different stages in a process.	T2(21) to produce simple flow charts or diagrams that explain a process
11	10	Plan a sustained story using the main components of story writing: characters, setting, plot.	T3(10) to write sustained stories, using their knowledge of story elements: narrative, settings, characterisation, dialogue and the language of story
12	11	To create a class poetry anthology.	T3(8) …to classify poems into simple types; to make class anthologies
13	12	Write a non-fiction report organized with sub-headings.	T3(20) to write non-fiction texts, using texts read as models for own writing, sub-headings, captions
14	13	Make simple notes from a non-fiction text.	T3(16) to scan a text to find specific sections, e.g. key words or phrases
15	14	Write simple evaluations of fiction books.	T3(12) to write simple evaluations of books read and discussed, giving reasons
16	14	Write simple evaluations of non-fiction books.	T3(12) to write simple evaluations of books read and discussed, giving reasons

Expected outcomes and key text level objectives

Book 1 Year 3

Writing Frame	Unit	Expected outcome	Key text level objective
17	1	Write short descriptions based on real and imagined places.	T1(11) to develop the use of settings in own stories by: writing short descriptions of known places; writing a description in the style of a familiar story
18	2	Write a passage of dialogue using correct speech punctuation.	T1(10) to use reading as a model to write own passages of dialogue
19	3	Write a story opening that engages the reader's interest.	T1(11) to investigate and collect sentences/phrases for story openings and endings – use some of these formal elements in retelling and story writing
20	4	Write a shape poem.	T1(13) to invent calligrams and a range of shape poems, selecting appropriate words and careful presentation. Build up class collections
21	5	Write a simple playscript.	T1(14) to write simple playscripts based on own reading and oral work
22	6	To make notes using headings to locate information and identifying key words and phrases.	T1(20) to…identify main points of text, e.g. by noting or underlining key words or phrases
23	7	Write a non-chronological report from known information using a writing frame.	T1(22) to write simple non-chronological reports from known information, e.g. from own experience
24	8	Plan a simple story structure; sequence the key incidents in a diagrammatic form.	T2(7) to describe and sequence key incidents in a variety of ways, e.g. by listing, charting, mapping, making simple storyboards
25	9	Plan a portrait of a fictional character.	T2(8) to write portraits of characters, using story text to describe behaviours and characteristics
26	10	Plan and write an alternative sequel to a traditional story.	T2(10) to write alternative sequels to traditional stories using same characters and settings
27	11	Write new verses for a poem using a given structure.	T2(11) write new or extended verses for performance based on models
28	12	Write simple instructions using a range of organizational devices.	T2(16) to write simple instructions…using a range of organisational devices, e.g. lists, dashes, commas for lists in sentences
29	13	Make notes of key points in non-fiction extracts.	T2(17) to make clear notes, through, e.g.…making use of simple formats to capture key points, e.g. flow chart, 'for' and 'against' columns, matrices etc.
30	14	Present key points using a flow chart format.	T2(17) to make clear notes, through, e.g.…making use of simple formats to capture key points, e.g. flow chart, 'for' and 'against' columns, matrices etc.
31	15	Plan a short story using language to create an effect: fear, amusement or pity.	T3(11) to write openings to stories or chapters linked to or arising from reading; to focus on language to create effects, e.g. building tension, suspense, creating moods, setting scenes
32	16	Write a first person account about familiar subjects.	T3(12) to write a first person account, e.g. write a character's own account of an incident in a story read
33	17	Write book reviews for a friend, based on evaluations of plot, characters and language.	T3(14) to write book reviews for a specified audience, based on evaluations of plot, characters and language
34	18	Plan a poem using onomatopoeia.	T3(15) to write poetry that uses sound to create effects, e.g. onomatopoeia, alliteration, distinctive rhymes
35	19	Plan and write a letter using standard letter-writing conventions.	T3(20) to write letters, notes and messages linked to work in other subjects…selecting style and vocabulary appropriate to the intended reader
36	20	Write about the same event in two different ways: in the form of a news report and a letter.	T3(22) experiment with recounting the same event in a variety of ways, e.g. in the form of a story, a letter, a news report
37	21	Make a page for an information book, setting the information out in alphabetical order.	T3(24) to make alphabetically ordered texts – use information from other subjects, own experience, or derived from other information books
38	22	Identify key words in a non-fiction text.	T3(25) to revise and extend work on note-making from previous term

Expected outcomes and key text level objectives

Book 2 Year 4

Writing Frame	Unit	Expected outcome	Key text level objective
39	1	To write character profiles evoking different responses in the reader.	T1(11) write character sketches, focusing on small details to evoke sympathy or dislike
40	2	Write about a frightening situation based on personal experience.	T1(12) to write independently, linking own experience to situations in historical stories, e.g. How would I have responded? What would I do next?
41	3	Use playscript conventions, such as setting the characters' names to the left; include stage directions.	T1(13) to write playscripts, e.g. using known stories as basis
42	4	Write an animal poem linked to other animal poems read; focus on descriptive words and phrases, using a word web as a starting point.	T1(14) to write poems based on personal or imagined experience, linked to poems read. List brief phrases and words; experiment with powerful and expressive verbs
43	5	Plan newspaper style reports; create newspaper headlines.	T1(24) to write newspaper style reports…including: composing headlines; using IT to draft and lay out reports; editing stories to fit a particular space; organising writing into paragraphs
44	6	Write a set of instructions for different purposes.	T1(25) to write clear instructions using conventions learned from reading
45	7	Write a report about a personal hobby.	T1(26) to improve the cohesion of written instructions and directions through the use of link phrases and organisational devices such as sub-headings and numbering
46	8	Plan a descriptive passage about an imaginary world.	T2(10) to develop use of settings in own writing, making use of work on adjectives and figurative language to describe settings effectively
47	9	Write a rhyming poem about an historical or mythical event, incorporating some archaic words.	T2(11) to write poetry based on the structure and/or style of poems read, e.g. taking account of vocabulary, archaic expressions, patterns of rhyme, choruses, similes
48	10	Write descriptive passages about imaginary landscapes.	T2(10) to develop use of settings in own writing, making use of work on adjectives and figurative language to describe settings effectively
49	11	Write a story continuation; edit and redraft the story to improve it.	T2(14) notemaking: to edit down a sentence or passage by deleting the less important elements, e.g. repetitions, asides, secondary considerations, and discuss the reasons for editorial choices
50	12	Make notes (key words and phrases) and use them to write a summary of information.	T2(22) to fill out brief notes into connected prose
51	13	Write an explanation about a social phenomenon.	T2(25) to write explanations…using conventions identified through reading
52	14	Write an explanation of a cyclical process, incorporating labelled diagrams.	T2(23) to collect information from a variety of sources and present it in one simple format, e.g. wall chart, labelled diagram
53	15	Write from the point of view of a fictional character, demonstrating empathy.	T3(11) to explore the main issues of a story by writing about a dilemma and the issues it raises for a character
54	16	Write an alternative ending for a known story.	T3(12) to write an alternative ending for a known story and discuss how this would change the reader's view of the characters and events in the original story
55	17	Plan and write a haiku poem.	T3(15) to produce polished poetry through revision, e.g. deleting words, adding words, changing words, reorganising words and lines, experimenting with figurative language
56	18	Plan and write an acrostic poem.	T3(15) to produce polished poetry through revision, e.g. deleting words, adding words, changing words, reorganising words and lines, experimenting with figurative language
57	19	Write a persuasive argument, presenting a clear point of view about a social issue.	T3(22) to use writing frames if necessary to back up points of view with illustrations and examples
58	20	Write an argument, presenting a clear point of view in the context of a letter.	T3(23) to present a point of view in writing, e.g. in the form of a letter, a report or a script, linking points persuasively and selecting style and vocabulary appropriate to the reader
59	21	Produce an eye-catching and informative advertisement.	T3(23) to present a point of view in writing, e.g. in the form of a letter, a report or a script, linking points persuasively and selecting style and vocabulary appropriate to the reader
60	22	Summarize a non-fiction passage including key words and phrases.	T3(24) to summarise in writing the key ideas from, e.g. a paragraph or chapter

Expected outcomes and key text level objectives

Book 3 Year 5

Writing Frame	Unit	Expected outcome	Key text level objective
61	1	Produce a front and back cover for a book, including a story synopsis.	T1(13) to record ideas, reflections and predictions about a book, e.g. through a reading log or journal
62	2	Write a continuation of a story in the manner of the writer.	T1(15) to write new scenes or characters into a story, in the manner of the writer, maintaining consistency of character and style, using paragraphs to organise and develop detail
63	3	Plan a poem using similes and metaphors.	T1(17) to write metaphors from original ideas or from similes
64	4	Write the opening scene of a playscript.	T1(18) write own playscript, applying conventions learned from reading
65	5	Plan appropriate costumes, props and set design for a playscript.	T1(18) write own playscript, applying conventions learned from reading; including production notes
66	6	Write a recount in the style of a magazine report.	T1(24) to write recounts based on subject, topic or personal experiences for (a) a close friend and (b) an unknown reader, e.g. an account of a field trip, a match, a historical event
67	7	Write a recount in the style of a police statement.	T1(24) to write recounts based on subject, topic or personal experiences for (a) a close friend and (b) an unknown reader, e.g. an account of a field trip, a match, a historical event
68	8	Write instructions to accompany a diagram.	T1(25) to write instructional texts, and test them out, e.g. instructions for loading computers, design briefs for technology, rules for games
69	9	Write notes for a talk on a subject of personal interest.	T1(26) to make notes for different purposes, e.g. noting key points as a record of what has been read, listing cues for a talk, and to build on these notes in their own writing or speaking
70	10	Plan a fable using structures and themes identified in reading.	T2(11) to write own version of legends, myths and fables, using structures and themes identified in reading
71	11	Plan a piece of writing with a particular audience in mind.	T2(13) to review and edit writing to produce a final form, matched to the needs of an identified reader
72	12	Write an additional verse for a narrative poem.	T2(12) to use the structures of poems to write extensions based on these, e.g. additional verses, or substituting own words and ideas
73	13	Make notes and use them to write an explanation or report in the third person.	T2(22) to plan, compose, edit and refine short non-chronological reports and explanatory texts, using reading as a source, focusing on clarity, conciseness and impersonal style
74	14	Make notes that explain a viewpoint, taking into account both advantages and disadvantages.	T2(22) to plan, compose, edit and refine short non-chronological reports and explanatory texts, using reading as a source, focusing on clarity, conciseness and impersonal style
75	15	Create notes from information texts, acknowledging sources appropriately.	T2(23) to record and acknowledge sources in their own writing
76	16	Plan and write about a given scenario from the perspective of a fictional character.	T3(7) to write from another character's point of view, e.g. retelling an incident in letter form
77	17	Plan and write a dialogue between two fictional characters.	T3(9) to write in the style of an author, e.g. writing on to complete a section...writing additional dialogue
78	18	Keep a reading journal including personal comments and reflections about the story.	T3(10) to write discursively about a novel or story, e.g. to describe, explain, or comment on it
79	19	Write a formal, persuasive letter about a local issue.	T3(17) to draft and write individual, group or class letters for real purposes, e.g. to put a point of view, comment on an emotive issue, protest; to edit and present to finished state
80	20	Write a report about an event in two different styles: a factual newspaper report and a persuasive editorial.	T3(18) to write a commentary on an issue on paper or screen (e.g. as a news editorial...) setting out and justifying a personal view
81	21	Present an argument expressing different viewpoints.	T3(19) to construct an argument in note form or full text to persuade others of a point of view and: present the case to the class or group; evaluate its effectiveness
82	22	Prepare a leaflet that persuades the reader to accept a particular viewpoint, or to buy a particular product.	T3(18) to write a commentary on an issue on paper or screen (e.g. as a news editorial, leaflet), setting out and justifying a personal view; to use structures from reading to set out and link points, e.g. numbered lists, bullet points

Expected outcomes and key text level objectives

Book 4 Year 6

Writing Frame	Unit	Expected outcome	Key text level objective
83	1	Plan a story focusing specifically on the plot, characters and structure.	T1(7) to plan quickly and effectively the plot, characters and structure of their own narrative writing
84	2	Summarize a passage of text.	T1(8) to summarise a passage, chapter or text in a specified number of words
85	3	Prepare a short extract from a classic story by a long-established author as a playscript.	T1(9) to prepare a short section of story as a script, e.g. using stage directions, location/setting
86	4	Plan a modern retelling of a well-known story using the same identified themes.	T1(6) to manipulate narrative perspective by…producing a modern retelling
87	5	Plan a poem experimenting with active verbs and personification.	T1(10) to write own poems experimenting with active verbs and personification
88	6	To present information using a curriculum vitae format.	T1(14) to develop the skills of biographical and autobiographical writing in role, adopting distinctive voices, e.g. of historical characters through, e.g. preparing a CV etc.
89	7	Explore different ways of presenting factual reports and evaluate their usefulness.	T1(17) to write non-chronological reports linked to other subjects
90	8	Plan and write a report on an imagined event using the styles and conventions of journalism.	T1(16) to use the styles and conventions of journalism to report on e.g. real or imagined events
91	9	Write alternative story endings, evoking different responses, using appropriate story writing conventions.	T2(10) to use different genres as models to write, e.g. short extracts, sequels, additional episodes, alternative endings, using appropriate conventions, language
92	10	To plan a dream sequence.	T2(11) to write own story using, e.g. a story within a story
93	11	Plan and write a story evoking a humorous response.	T2(12) to study in depth one genre and produce an extended piece of similar writing
94	12	To plan and write an effective argument, supporting and illustrating points persuasively.	T2(18) to construct effective arguments: developing a point logically and effectively; supporting and illustrating points persuasively
95	13	Write a newspaper report that presents a balanced argument.	T2(18) to construct effective arguments: developing a point logically and effectively; supporting and illustrating points persuasively; anticipating possible objections
96	14	Design an application form for membership to a club using the characteristic features of official forms.	T2(20) to discuss the way standard English varies in different contexts, e.g.:…why questionnaires must be specific
97	15	Plan poems designed to evoke particular responses.	T3(13) to write a sequence of poems linked by theme or form
98	16	Write a blurb for the back cover of a book including a brief synopsis of the plot.	T3(10) to write a brief synopsis of a text, e.g. for back cover blurb
99	17	Write a personal response to a text, including information such as title, author, main characters and a brief summary of the plot.	T3(8) to use a reading journal effectively to raise and refine personal responses to a text and prepare for discussion
100	18	Plan additional chapters to a story.	T3(14) to write an extended story, worked on over time on a theme identified in reading
101	19	Write an instructional text or a factual description.	T3(20) to secure control of impersonal writing, particularly the sustained use of the present tense and the passive voice
102	20	Divide a whole text into paragraphs; write a chapter for an information book divided into sections with sub-headings.	T3(21) to divide whole texts into paragraphs, paying attention to the sequence of paragraphs and to the links between one paragraph and the next, e.g. through the choice of appropriate connectives
103	21	Plan research for writing for a selected purpose.	T3(17) to appraise text quickly and effectively; to retrieve information from it; to find information quickly and evaluate its value
104	22	Present similar information in a variety of different ways.	T3(22) to select the appropriate style and form to suit a specific purpose and audience, drawing on knowledge of different non-fiction text types

Planning a story

| Name _____ | **Writing Frame 1** |

I was on my way to school on _____

_____

The weather was _____

_____

I was feeling _____

_____

_____

Then, _____

_____

_____

The next thing I knew, _____

_____

_____

When I told my teacher, she said _____

_____

Writing Frame for Introductory Book, Unit 1   *Focus on Writing* © John Jackman and Wendy Wren, HarperCollins*Publishers* 1998
Revised edition 2004

Writing a story

Name _____

Writing Frame
2

My picture story will be about
_____

Writing Frame for Introductory Book, Unit 2

Writing a story

Name _____

Writing Frame 3

A story about something that happened to me

My story will be about when:

_____
_____
_____
_____

These people and animals will be in my story:

_____
_____
_____

My story will happen at:

_____
_____
_____

Writing poems

Name _____

Writing Frame
4

Can you tell whether my pet is real or pretend?

My pet's name is _____

My pet is a _____

When _____ was 1
_____

When _____ was 2
_____

When _____ was 3
_____

When _____ was 4
_____

When _____ was 5
_____

Can you tell whether _____ is real or pretend?

Writing Frame for Introductory Book, Unit 3   *Focus on Writing* © John Jackman and Wendy Wren, HarperCollins*Publishers* 1998
Revised edition 2004

Ordering

Name _____

Writing Frame 5

This is how to _____

This is what you will need.

_____   _____

_____   _____

_____   _____

This is what to do.

1. _____
2. _____
3. _____
4. _____

My picture of

Writing Frame for Introductory Book, Unit 4 *Focus on Writing* © John Jackman and Wendy Wren, HarperCollins*Publishers* 1998
Revised edition 2004

Instructions

Name _____

Writing Frame
6

This is how to get from _____

to _____

Here is a map of my journey.

Here are the directions.

First, _____

Next, _____

After that _____

_____

_____

_____

Writing Frame for Introductory Book, Unit 5

Story settings

Name _____

Writing Frame 7

I am going to write a story about
_____

My story will happen at
_____

Here is a picture of where my story will happen.

Lists of words I might use about where and when my story will happen.

_____   _____
_____   _____
_____   _____
_____   _____
_____   _____

Who's in the story?

Name _____

Writing Frame 8

I am going to write a story about
_____

The people and animals in my story will be:

Name: _____

Describing words I will use:

_____
_____
_____
_____

Picture:

Name: _____

Describing words I will use:

_____
_____
_____
_____

Picture:

Writing Frame for Introductory Book, Unit 7   Focus on Writing © John Jackman and Wendy Wren, HarperCollins*Publishers* 1998
Revised edition 2004

Making a dictionary

Name _____

Writing Frame 9

My dictionary page is about _____

Word   **Picture**   **Meaning**

Writing Frame for Introductory Book, Unit 8 — *Focus on Writing* © John Jackman and Wendy Wren, HarperCollins*Publishers* 1998
Revised edition 2004

Diagrams

Name _____

Writing Frame 10

This is a diagram of _____

The diagram shows:

1. _____
2. _____
3. _____
4. _____

Writing Frame for Introductory Book, Unit 9 *Focus on Writing* © John Jackman and Wendy Wren, HarperCollins*Publishers* 1998
Revised edition 2004

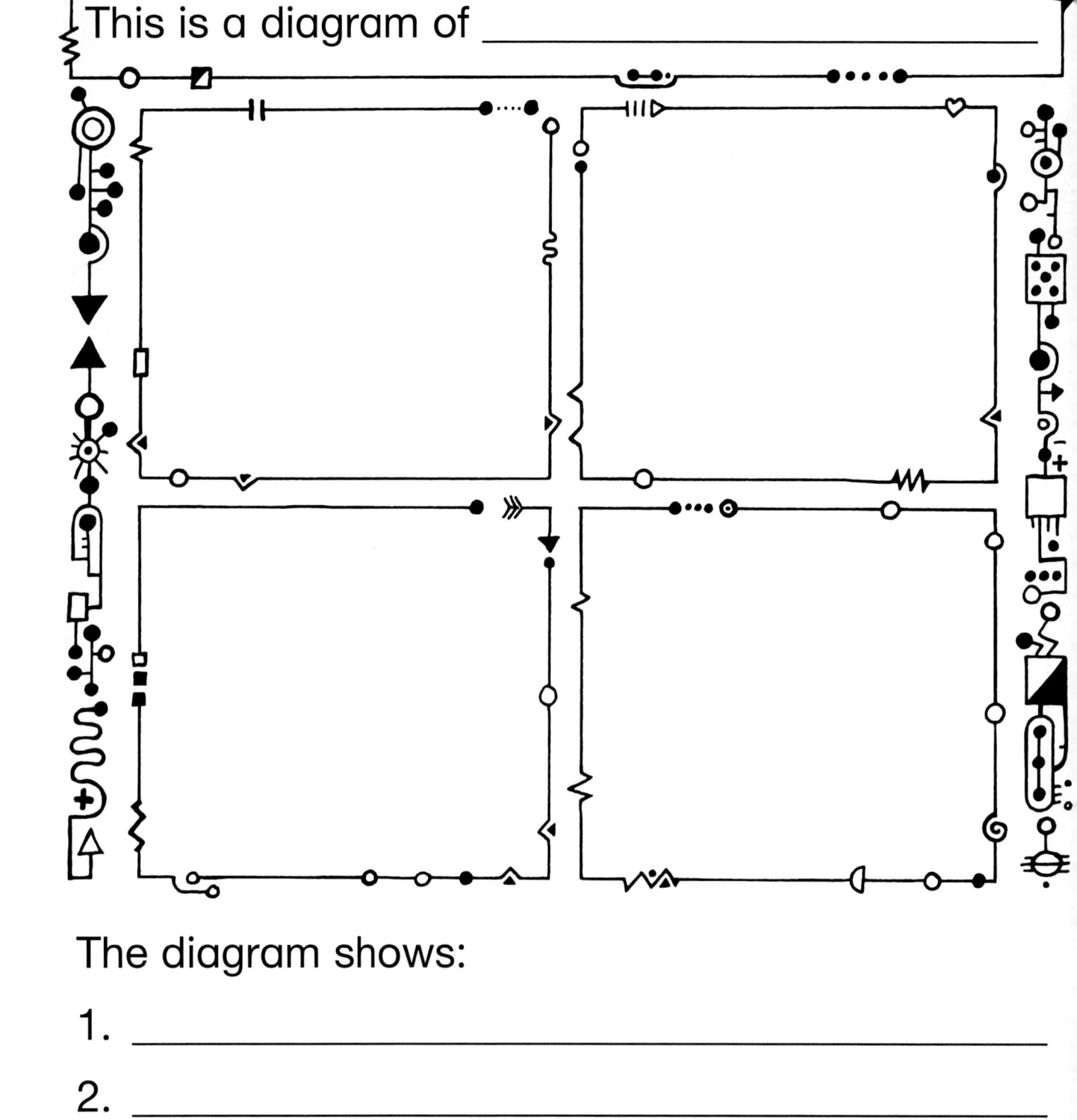

Writing longer stories

Name _____

Writing Frame 11

This is my story plan for a story about
_____

Where and when the story will happen

Who will be in the story

What will happen
- At the beginning

- In the middle

- At the end

Writing Frame for Introductory Book, Unit 10

Riddles and funny poems

Name _____

Writing Frame 12

My favourite Funny Poem

Title _____

Poet _____

Writing Frame for Introductory Book, Unit 11 *Focus on Writing* © John Jackman and Wendy Wren, HarperCollins*Publishers* 1998
Revised edition 2004

Writing a report

Name _____

Writing Frame 13

Keeping a _____ as a pet

Feeding

....
....
....
....

Keeping it clean

....
....
....
....

Exercising it

....
....
....
....

Writing Frame for Introductory Book, Unit 12 *Focus on Writing* © John Jackman and Wendy Wren, HarperCollins*Publishers* 1998
Revised edition 2004

Making notes

Name _____

Writing Frame 14

Polar bears

The frozen sea around the North Pole is polar bear country. The bears live at the edge of the ice, where it meets the sea.

Good swimmers

The polar bears have strong, partly webbed front paws, which help make them good swimmers. They can stay underwater for up to two minutes.

Hunters

Each bear needs to catch and eat one seal every 11 days. It will sit for hours next to a seal's breathing hole in the ice, waiting for one to come up for air. Then it will pounce. These bears also eat seabirds, fish and crabs.

Writing Frame for Introductory Book, Unit 13   Focus on Writing © John Jackman and Wendy Wren, HarperCollins*Publishers* 1998
Revised edition 2004

Thinking about books

Name _____   **Writing Frame 15**

I enjoyed reading this storybook.

Title: ....

Author: ....

Illustrator: ....

The story happens at:

....

....

The main characters are:

....

....

The story is about:

....

....

The best thing about this book is:

....

....

Writing Frame for Introductory Book, Unit 14   *Focus on Writing* © John Jackman and Wendy Wren, HarperCollins*Publishers* 1998
Revised edition 2004

Thinking about books

Name _____

Writing Frame 16

I enjoyed reading this information book.

Title: ....

Author: ....

Illustrator: ....

This book is about:

....

....

The main thing I learnt was:

....

....

The best thing about this book is:

....

....

The worst thing about this book is:

....

....

Writing Frame for Introductory Book, Unit 14 *Focus on Writing* © John Jackman and Wendy Wren, HarperCollins*Publishers* 1998
Revised edition 2004

Story settings

Name _____

Writing Frame 17

_____

_____

_____

Writing Frame for Book 1, Unit 1 Focus on Writing © John Jackman and Wendy Wren, HarperCollinsPublishers 1998
Revised edition 2004

Using spoken words in stories

Name _____

Writing Frame 18

_____, he said.

_____, she replied.

Writing Frame for Book 1, Unit 2

Focus on Writing © John Jackman and Wendy Wren, HarperCollins*Publishers* 1998
Revised edition 2004

Story openings

Name _____

Writing Frame 19

It was Christmas Eve, _____
_____
_____
_____
_____
_____

"Do you realise," said Ethel, _____
_____
_____
_____
_____
_____
_____

Writing Frame for Book 1, Unit 3

Shape poems

Name _____

Writing Frame 20

Writing Frame for Book 1, Unit 4   *Focus on Writing* © John Jackman and Wendy Wren, HarperCollins*Publishers* 1998
Revised edition 2004

Turning a story into a play

Name _____

Writing Frame 21

Scene _____

Character's name

Stage direction (----------------)

(----------------)

Writing Frame for Book 1, Unit 5

Focus on Writing © John Jackman and Wendy Wren, HarperCollins*Publishers* 1998
Revised edition 2004

Giving information

Name _____

Writing Frame
22

♦ Cooker

This is used to cook and heat our meals. Some cookers use gas and some use electricity. A few use both gas and electricity.

♦ Electric kettle

Inside the kettle is a wire inside a tube. This is called the element. It gets hot and heats the water inside the kettle until it boils. The outside of a kettle can get very hot.

♦ Toaster

A toaster has elements too. The lever on the side turns the element on, and a catch inside the toaster turns it off when the bread is toasted. Never put anything except bread in a toaster.

♦ Fridge and freezer

Food goes bad more quickly if it isn't kept cool. An electric motor makes the air inside a fridge cooler so the food stays fresh for a few days. In freezers the air is very cold, to make the food freeze and stay fresh for a few weeks.

♦ Washing machine

Electricity works the motor that turns the drum and heats the water.

♦ Iron

The element is inside, so a hot and cold iron look exactly the same, so never touch an iron or it may burn you badly!

Writing Frame for Book 1, Unit 6

Focus on Writing © John Jackman and Wendy Wren, HarperCollins*Publishers* 1998
Revised edition 2004

Writing a report

Name _____

Writing Frame 23

On _____ _____

went to _____

There was _____

_____

_____

The thing we enjoyed most was ____

_____

_____

We also liked _____

_____

I wish we could _____

_____

It had been _____

_____

Writing Frame for Book 1, Unit 7

Focus on Writing © John Jackman and Wendy Wren, HarperCollins*Publishers* 1998
Revised edition 2004

A story plan

Name _____

Writing Frame 24

Characters
Who is in the story

Setting
Where and when the story takes place

Plot
Beginning

Middle

End

Writing Frame for Book 1, Unit 8

Focus on Writing © John Jackman and Wendy Wren, HarperCollins*Publishers* 1998
Revised edition 2004

Characters in stories

Name _____

Writing Frame 25

Good character

Bad character

Appearance and characteristics

Writing Frame for Book 1, Unit 9

Focus on Writing © John Jackman and Wendy Wren, HarperCollins*Publishers* 1998
Revised edition 2004

Continuing a story

Name _____

Writing Frame 26

Arthur pulled the sword out of the stone. Sir Ector said: "You are king of England." Then one of the knights cried: "We don't want Arthur to be king!"

What happened next?
Write your own ending.

_____
_____
_____
_____
_____
_____
_____
_____

Writing Frame for Book 1, Unit 10

Poetry

Name _____

Writing Frame 27

It's full of the moon

The dogs dance out

Through _____ and _____

and _____.

They _____ and _____

And _____ and _____.

They _____ _____ _____.

They _____ through _____.

They _____ through _____.

They_____ and _____

and _____.

They _____ around and _____ around

With _____ in their _____.

They _____ in the meadow.

They _____ on the lawn.

Tonight's the night

The dogs dance out

And chase their tails till dawn.

Writing Frame for Book 1, Unit 11

Focus on Writing © John Jackman and Wendy Wren, HarperCollins*Publishers* 1998
Revised edition 2004

Instructions

Name _____

Writing Frame 28

Object of the game

Number of players

Equipment

Plan of game

How to play

Writing Frame for Book 1, Unit 12

Focus on Writing © John Jackman and Wendy Wren, HarperCollins*Publishers* 1998
Revised edition 2004

Key words

| **Name** _____ | **Writing Frame 29** |

Subject:

Writing Frame for Book 1, Unit 13 *Focus on Writing* © John Jackman and Wendy Wren, HarperCollins*Publishers* 1998
Revised edition 2004

Using key points

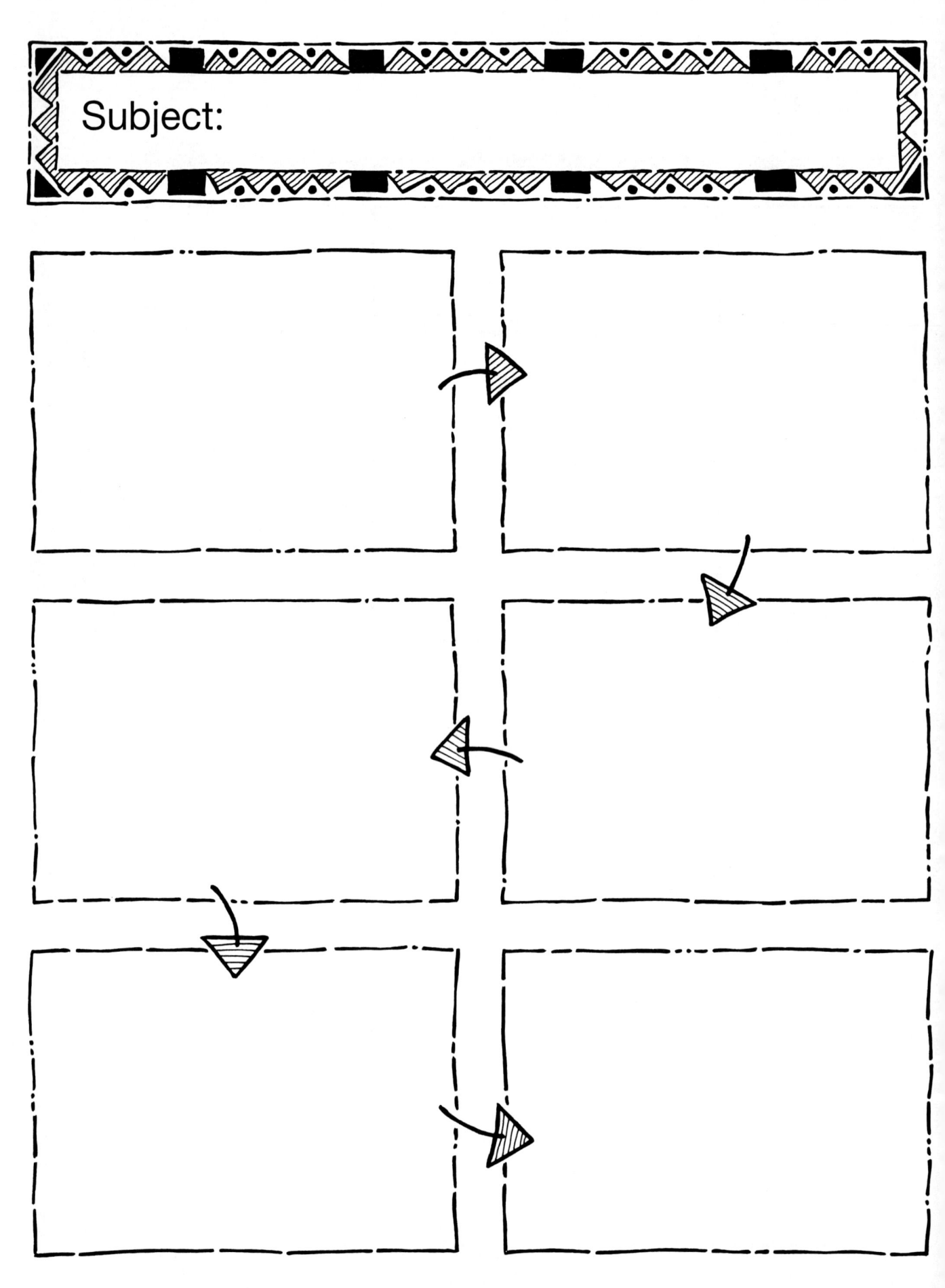

Name _____

Writing Frame
30

Subject:

Writing Frame for Book 1, Unit 14

Focus on Writing © John Jackman and Wendy Wren, HarperCollins*Publishers* 1998
Revised edition 2004

How stories make you feel

Name _____

Writing Frame 31

_____
_____
_____
_____
_____

Frightening

Funny

Sad

Writing Frame for Book 1, Unit 15   *Focus on Writing* © John Jackman and Wendy Wren, HarperCollins*Publishers* 1998
Revised edition 2004

Writing about myself

Name _____

Writing Frame 32

I am

_____

My favourite things are

_____

Yesterday I

_____

When I

_____

Soon I

Writing Frame for Book 1, Unit 16

Book reviews

Name _____

Writing Frame 33

Title _____

Author _____

Publisher _____

Characters

_____

Setting

_____

Plot

_____

My opinion

Writing Frame for Book 1, Unit 17

Sound poetry

Name _____

Writing Frame 34

walking through autumn leaves:

washing machine:

eating crisps:

Writing a letter

Name _____

Writing Frame 35

Writing Frame for Book 1, Unit 19

Focus on Writing © John Jackman and Wendy Wren, HarperCollins*Publishers* 1998
Revised edition 2004

A news report

Name _____

Writing Frame 36

Heading

From _____

Late last night _____

_____

_____

_____

It was just after _____

when _____

_____

_____

_____

_____

_____

_____

_____

Picture

Meanwhile _____

_____

_____

_____

_____

_____

_____

Writing Frame for Book 1, Unit 20

Alphabetical order

Name _____

Writing Frame
37

Subject:

Words:

Writing Frame for Book 1, Unit 21

Focus on Writing © John Jackman and Wendy Wren, HarperCollins*Publishers* 1998
Revised edition 2004

Keeping a dog is a big responsibility.

There are many different kinds of dogs; some are kept only as pets, but some do important work, such as police dogs, sniffer dogs and sheep dogs.

All dogs need company and exercise. Bigger dogs, such as Alsatians and Great Danes, need much more exercise than smaller dogs like Chihuahuas and Yorkshire Terriers. Dogs need exercise every day. They should be taken for a walk on a lead, until they are in an area where it is free from traffic and safe. Then they can be let off the lead.

Wild dogs, such as foxes and wolves, hunt other animals for food. Tame dogs like to eat meat too, so dogs can be expensive pets to keep. Some vets say that about half the food a dog eats should be meat. The other half should be bread or cereal and dog biscuits. A full-grown dog needs one meal a day, and should always have a bowl of fresh water to drink. Dogs enjoy gnawing large bones, but should never be given bones that crack and splinter, like chicken bones.

A dog can sleep outdoors in a kennel, provided it is dry and large enough for the dog to move around. Straw makes good bedding, but it should be changed each week. If your dog is kept indoors in a dog basket, it should have a blanket that is washed whenever it is dirty.

Dogs should be brushed each day and given a bath regularly with warm water and dog soap. Sometimes they may need to be sprayed to kill any fleas. All dogs need to be taken to the vet for regular injections to protect them against certain dog illnesses.

If you can do all these things, and your home is big enough for a dog, then you will be a good owner and you will have a happy and contented pet.

Thinking about characters

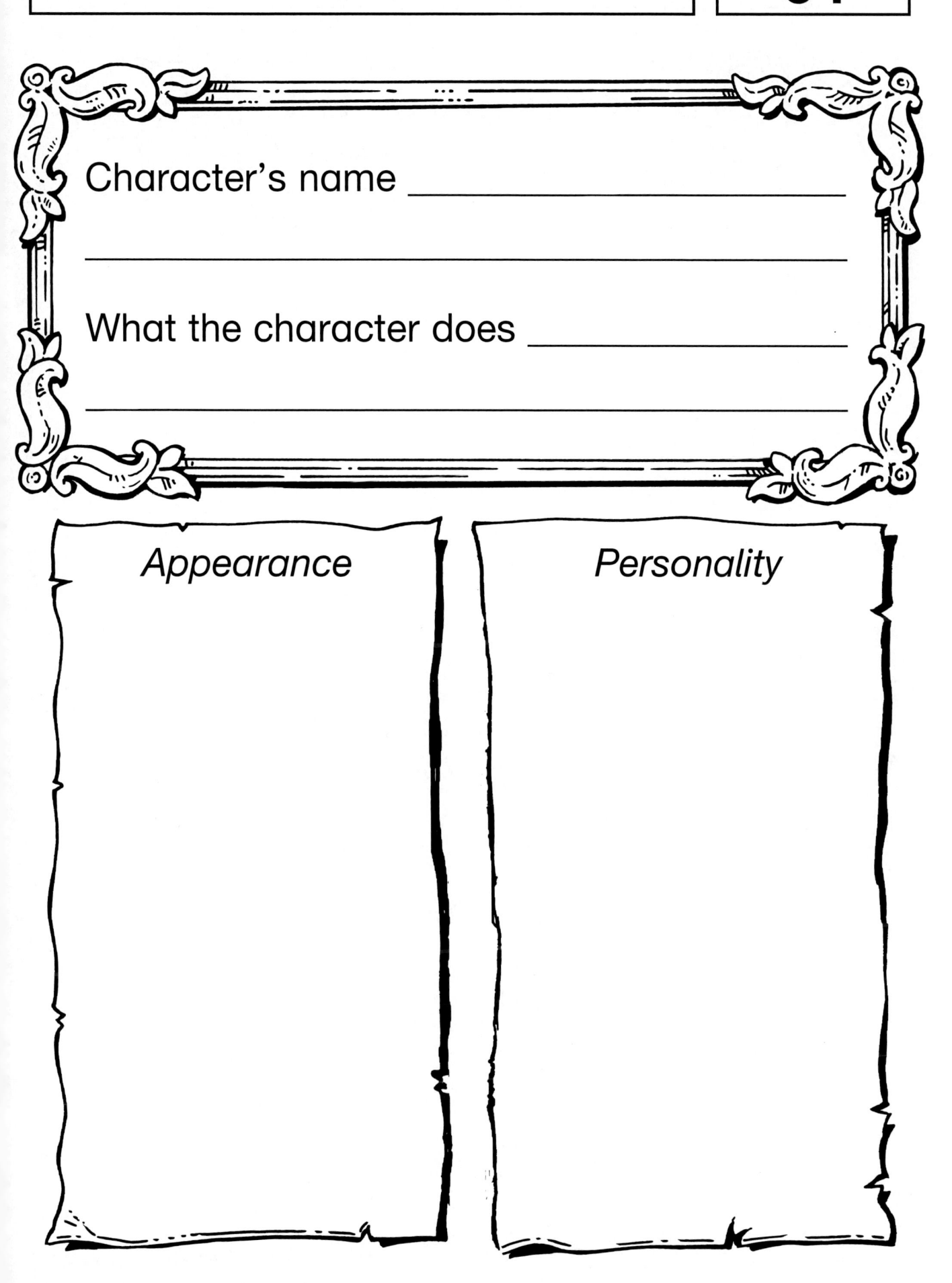

Name _____

Writing Frame 39

Character's name _____
_____

What the character does _____
_____

Appearance

Personality

Writing Frame for Book 2, Unit 1

Focus on Writing © John Jackman and Wendy Wren, HarperCollins*Publishers* 1998
Revised edition 2004

Taking a character's place

Name _____

Writing Frame 40

Imagine you are in...

...a frightening situation.

What would you do?

...a dangerous situation.

What would you do?

Writing Frame for Book 2, Unit 2

Focus on Writing © John Jackman and Wendy Wren, HarperCollins*Publishers* 1998
Revised edition 2004

Writing a playscript

Name _____

Writing Frame 41

Susan and Tim have found a strange bad-tempered creature in their garden. It looks like a frog but it can talk.

Scene _____

Stage direction (_____)

Character's name

Writing Frame for Book 2, Unit 3

Poetry topics

Name _____

Writing Frame 42

My dog

Your dog

My cat

Your cat

Writing Frame for Book 2, Unit 4

Focus on Writing © John Jackman and Wendy Wren, HarperCollins*Publishers* 1998
Revised edition 2004

Writing a newspaper report

Name _____

Writing Frame 43

The event _____
_____
_____

Date/time _____

Location/weather _____
_____

Purpose _____
_____

Activities (facts) _____
_____
_____
_____
_____

Activities (comments) _____
_____
_____

Writing Frame for Book 2, Unit 5

Focus on Writing © John Jackman and Wendy Wren, HarperCollinsPublishers 1998
Revised edition 2004

Writing instructions

Name _____

Writing Frame 44

Instructions for making

_____

You will need

- _____
- _____
- _____
- _____
- _____

Diagram/picture

What to do

1. _____
2. _____
3. _____
4. _____
5. _____
6. _____
7. _____

Writing Frame for Book 2, Unit 6

Focus on Writing © John Jackman and Wendy Wren, HarperCollins*Publishers* 1998
Revised edition 2004

Organising reports

Name _____

Writing Frame 45

My hobby is _____

I like my hobby because _____

_____

_____

_____

The things I need for my hobby are:

- _____
- _____
- _____
- _____
- _____

To take up my hobby you need to:

_____

_____

A good book on this hobby is _____

_____

Writing Frame for Book 2, Unit 7   *Focus on Writing* © John Jackman and Wendy Wren, HarperCollins*Publishers* 1998
Revised edition 2004

Story settings

Name _____

Writing Frame 46

Smaug the Magnificent is a fierce dragon that lives inside a mountain. He guards a treasure which the dwarves and Bilbo Baggins are seeking.

How would you describe the mountain and the dragon?

Words and phrases to describe the mountain.

Words and phrases to describe the dragon.

Writing Frame for Book 2, Unit 8

Understanding poems from long ago

Name _____

Writing Frame 47

Think of a great deed for the king to do, and continue the poem to tell about it. Then say what happened to the spider.

Try to use some old-fashioned words and phrases.

The king _____
_____
_____
_____
_____

The spider _____
_____
_____
_____
_____

Writing Frame for Book 2, Unit 9   *Focus on Writing* © John Jackman and Wendy Wren, HarperCollins*Publishers* 1998
Revised edition 2004

More story settings

Name _____

Writing Frame **48**

Imagine you visit two very different planets.

The planet Zig is rather frightening.

Words and phrases to describe what the planet Zig looks like.

You feel safe on the planet Zog.

Words and phrases to describe what the planet Zog looks like.

Writing Frame for Book 2, Unit 10

Focus on Writing © John Jackman and Wendy Wren, HarperCollins*Publishers* 1998
Revised edition 2004

Editing

Name _____

Writing Frame 49

Sam has written a story about landing on the moon. All his sentences begin with 'It was' or 'I'.

Help Sam to improve his story by writing sentences that begin with these words and phrases:

Landing on the moon, _____
_____

Although _____
_____

Without warning, _____
_____

After a while _____
_____

Feeling tired, _____
_____

Suddenly, _____
_____

With a mighty roar _____
_____

Writing Frame for Book 2, Unit 11

Focus on Writing © John Jackman and Wendy Wren, HarperCollins*Publishers* 1998
Revised edition 2004

Making notes

Name _____

Writing Frame
50

Subject _____

Title and author of book used _____
_____

Key words and phrases
Paragraph 1
Paragraph 2
Paragraph 3
Paragraph 4

My shorter version _____
_____
_____
_____

Writing Frame for Book 2, Unit 12

Focus on Writing © John Jackman and Wendy Wren, HarperCollins*Publishers* 1998
Revised edition 2004

A written explanation

Name _____

Writing Frame 51

Subject _____

I am going to explain why _____
_____

There are several reasons for this, but the main one is _____
_____
_____

Another reason is _____
_____

A further reason is _____
_____

This is why I think that _____
_____
_____

Writing Frame for Book 2, Unit 13

Explaining how something works

Name _____

Writing Frame 52

Subject: _____

To begin with _____
_____

After this _____
_____

The next stage is _____
_____

Eventually _____
_____

Writing Frame for Book 2, Unit 14

Problems in stories

Name _____

Writing Frame 53

How would you feel if...

...you couldn't do something that everyone else was good at?

What would you do?

...someone got into trouble over something they didn't do and you knew who did it?

What would you do?

Writing Frame for Book 2, Unit 15

Focus on Writing © John Jackman and Wendy Wren, HarperCollins*Publishers* 1998
Revised edition 2004

A different ending

Name _____

Writing Frame 54

Ending 1

How do you want your reader to feel?

How would you end the story?

Ending 2

How do you want your reader to feel?

How would you end the story?

Writing haiku

Name _____

Writing Frame 55

Title _____

Words and phrases you could use.

1 syllable	2 syllables	3 syllables	More than 3 syllables

Your Haiku

___ ___ ___ ___ ___

___ ___ ___ ___ ___

___ ___ ___ ___ ___

Writing Frame for Book 2, Unit 17

Acrostic poems

Name _____

Writing Frame 56

Title _____

Words and phrases you can use.

Write your title downwards, one letter in each box.

☐ _____

☐ _____

☐ _____

☐ _____

☐ _____

☐ _____

☐ _____

Writing Frame for Book 2, Unit 18

Focus on Writing © John Jackman and Wendy Wren, HarperCollins*Publishers* 1998
Revised edition 2004

Points of view

Name _____

Writing Frame 57

Subject _____

Although not everyone would agree, I think that _____
_____

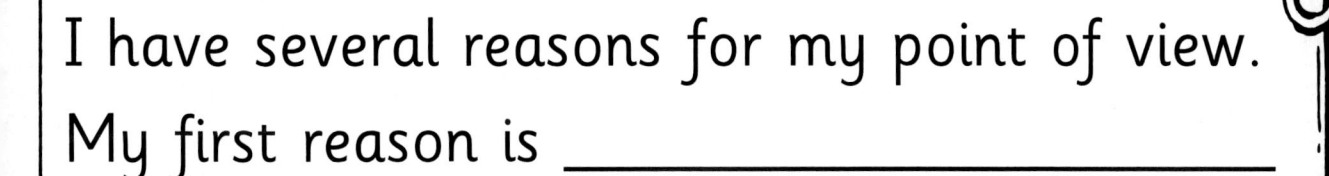

I have several reasons for my point of view. My first reason is _____
_____

A further reason is _____
_____

Therefore, although some people might say that _____
_____

I think I have shown that _____
_____

Writing Frame for Book 2, Unit 19

Focus on Writing © John Jackman and Wendy Wren, HarperCollins*Publishers* 1998
Revised edition 2004

Letter of complaint

Name _____

Writing Frame 58

Address _____
_____
_____
_____

Date _____

Dear _____

_____
_____
_____
_____
_____
_____
_____
_____

_____
_____

Writing Frame for Book 2, Unit 20

Looking at advertisements

Name _____

Writing Frame 59

says

Writing Frame for Book 2, Unit 21

Focus on Writing © John Jackman and Wendy Wren, HarperCollins*Publishers* 1998
Revised edition 2004

Making a summary

Name _____

Writing Frame 60

Subject _____

Title and author of book _____
_____

Key words and phrases

Paragraph 1

Paragraph 2

Paragraph 3

Paragraph 4

Paragraph 5

My summary

Writing Frame for Book 2, Unit 22

Focus on Writing © John Jackman and Wendy Wren, HarperCollins*Publishers* 1998
Revised edition 2004

Looking at book covers

| Name _____ | **Writing Frame 61** |

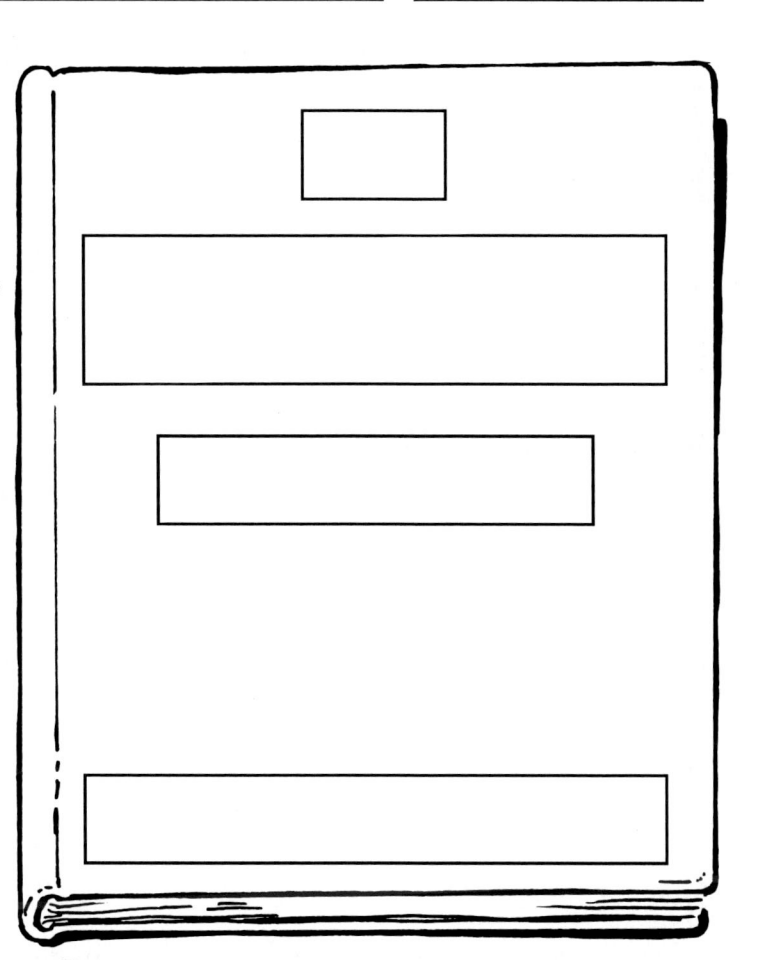

Front cover

publisher's logo ⇛→

book title ⇛→

author's name ⇛→

cover illustration ⇛→

comment by another author or from review/ details of prize ⇛→

Back cover
←⇚ summary of early part of the plot

←⇚ information about author

←⇚ other information

←⇚ price

ISBN 0-631-408
9 7034 16380

Writing Frame for Book 3, Unit 1   *Focus on Writing* © John Jackman and Wendy Wren, HarperCollins*Publishers* 1998
Revised edition 2004

Continuing a story

Name _____

Writing Frame 62

Characters in the story you have read

Some of the things that have happened in the story

What could happen next

Writing Frame for Book 3, Unit 2

Similes and metaphors

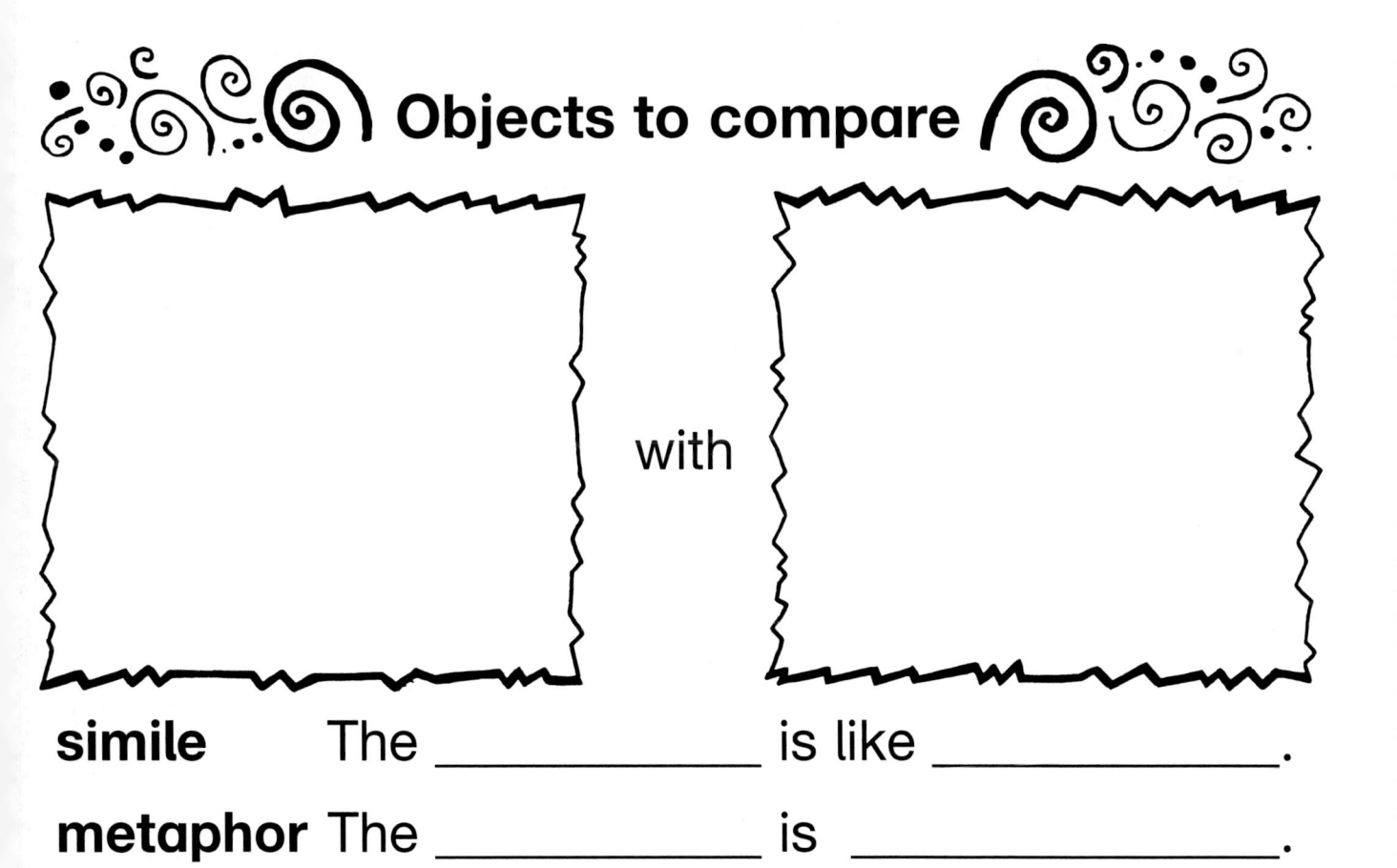

Name _____

Writing Frame 63

Objects to compare

[ ]   with   [ ]

simile   The _____ is like _____.
metaphor The _____ is _____.

Objects to compare

[ ]   with   [ ]

simile   The _____ is like _____.
metaphor The _____ is _____.

Stage directions

Name

Writing Frame 64

Scene 1: In the kitchen.

Mandy is making sandwiches. Philip enters stage left.

Philip: Going out, Mandy?

Mandy: (---)
_____
_____

Philip: (---)
_____
_____

Mandy: (---)
I'm in a hurry. I don't have time to chat.

Philip: (---)
Fine. I'm busy myself.

Mandy: (---)
_____
_____

Philip: (---)
_____
_____

Mandy: See you later, then.

Writing Frame for Book 3, Unit 4

Costumes, props and sets

Name _____

Writing Frame 65

Costumes

| Drawing | Notes | Drawing | Notes |

Props

| Drawing | Notes | Drawing | Notes |

Set

| Drawing | Notes |

Writing Frame for Book 3, Unit 5

Writing reports

Name _____

Writing Frame 66

The event _____
Date/time _____
Location/weather _____
Purpose _____
_____

Main highlights (facts)

1. _____
_____

2. _____
_____

3. _____
_____

Other facts _____
_____

Comments and opinions

_____
_____
_____
_____
_____

Writing Frame for Book 3, Unit 6 — *Focus on Writing* © John Jackman and Wendy Wren, HarperCollins*Publishers* 1998
Revised edition 2004

Different sorts of records

| Name _____ | Writing Frame **67** |

MIDSHIRE COUNTY CONSTABULARY

Reporting Officer: _____

Date of incident: _____

Time of incident: _____

Date reported: _____

Date statement taken: _____

Person who reported: _____

Address/location of incident: _____
_____

Statement of witness: _____
_____
_____
_____

Details of goods stolen/damaged: _____
_____
_____

Writing Frame for Book 3, Unit 7

Focus on Writing © John Jackman and Wendy Wren, HarperCollins*Publishers* 1998
Revised edition 2004

Writing instructions

Name _____

Writing Frame 68

Instructions for _____
_____

Equipment/materials

Diagram

_____
_____
_____
_____
_____

Instructions

_____
_____
_____
_____
_____
_____

Writing Frame for Book 3, Unit 8

Focus on Writing © John Jackman and Wendy Wren, HarperCollins*Publishers* 1998
Revised edition 2004

Notes for a talk, using abbreviations

Name _____

Writing Frame 69

Subject _____

Date of talk _____   Audience _____

Items to show _____
_____

Diagrams to help explain parts of the talk

Notes
Introduction _____
_____

Main part of talk _____
_____
_____
_____
_____

Close _____
_____

Writing Frame for Book 3, Unit 9

Focus on Writing © John Jackman and Wendy Wren, HarperCollins*Publishers* 1998
Revised edition 2004

Fables

Name _____

Writing Frame 70

The lesson of the fable

The characters

Where the fable takes place

What happens:
Beginning

Middle

End

Writing Frame for Book 3, Unit 10

Focus on Writing © John Jackman and Wendy Wren, HarperCollins*Publishers* 1998
Revised edition 2004

Writing for an audience

Name _____

Writing Frame 71

What you are writing

Who your audience is

Notes on the text

Notes on the illustrations

Other things to decide
- Vocabulary:
  simple ☐   difficult ☐   repetition ☐
- Captions ☐
- Paragraphs ☐
- Sections ☐

Writing Frame for Book 3, Unit 11

Focus on Writing © John Jackman and Wendy Wren, HarperCollins*Publishers* 1998
Revised edition 2004

Writing narrative poems

Name _____

Writing Frame **72**

The _____ **and the** _____

The _____ and the _____
went _____
 In a _____,
They took _____
and _____
 Wrapped up _____.
The _____ looked _____,
 And _____,
"Oh _____
 What a _____,
 _____
 _____
 What a _____!"

Writing Frame for Book 3, Unit 12

Focus on Writing © John Jackman and Wendy Wren, HarperCollins*Publishers* 1998
Revised edition 2004

Linking words and phrases

| **Name** _____ | **Writing Frame** **73** |

Subject _____

Sources of information _____
_____

Notes _____
_____
_____
_____

Sketches for diagrams or pictures

Draft account _____
_____
_____
_____
_____
_____
_____

Clear and concise explanations

Name _____

Writing Frame 74

Subject

Advantages

Disadvantages

Writing Frame for Book 3, Unit 14

Using Information

Name _____

Writing Frame 75

Subject _____

Author _____

Title _____

Publisher _____

Key facts _____
_____
_____
_____
_____

Author _____

Title _____

Publisher _____

Key facts _____
_____
_____
_____
_____

Writing Frame for Book 3, Unit 15

Focus on Writing © John Jackman and Wendy Wren, HarperCollins*Publishers* 1998
Revised edition 2004

Writing from a character's point of view

Name _____

Writing Frame 76

* The character's name

* What the character is like

* An incident in the story

* Writing about the incident as if I were that character

Dialogue

Name _____

Writing Frame 77

Who is having the conversation?

What are they talking about?

Type of conversation (choose one)
- ☐ argument
- ☐ discussion
- ☐ explanation
- ☐ chat   ☐ complaint

Words to use instead of 'said'.

The dialogue

Writing Frame for Book 3, Unit 17

Focus on Writing © John Jackman and Wendy Wren, HarperCollins*Publishers* 1998
Revised edition 2004

Writing about books

Name _____

Writing Frame **78**

Title _____

Author _____ Published by _____

The story takes place in

The main characters are

Some ideas in the story are

The episode I liked best was

because

I would or would not like my friends to read this book because

Letters to persuade

Name _____

Writing Frame 79

Address _____
_____
_____
_____

Date _____

Dear _____

_____
_____
_____
_____
_____
_____
_____

_____
_____

Writing Frame for Book 3, Unit 19

Focus on Writing © John Jackman and Wendy Wren, HarperCollins*Publishers* 1998
Revised edition 2004

Behind the news

Name _____

Writing Frame 80

_____ June _____   ___ p

_____

_____

_____ reports

Editorial

_____

_____

Writing Frame for Book 3, Unit 20   *Focus on Writing* © John Jackman and Wendy Wren, HarperCollins*Publishers* 1998
Revised edition 2004

Preparing an argument

Name _____

Writing Frame 81

Subject: _____

Opening: I am going to tell you why I think
_____

The main arguments for thinking this are:

1. _____
   _____

2. _____
   _____

3. _____
   _____

The main arguments against this are:

1. _____
   _____

2. _____
   _____

3. _____
   _____

Having carefully considered all the arguments, my conclusion is _____
_____
_____
_____

Writing Frame for Book 3, Unit 21

Leaflets to persuade

Name _____

Writing Frame 82

strong title/heading

main message

more detail

*   *

*   *

*   *

*   *

short, sharp conclusion

Story planning

Name _____   **Writing Frame 83**

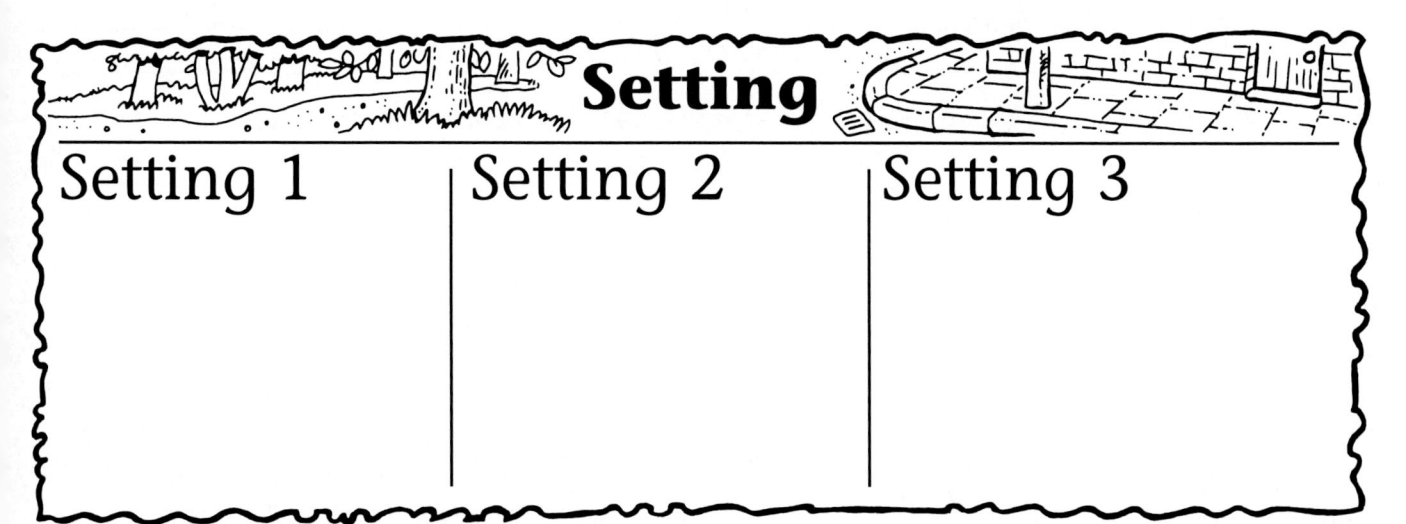

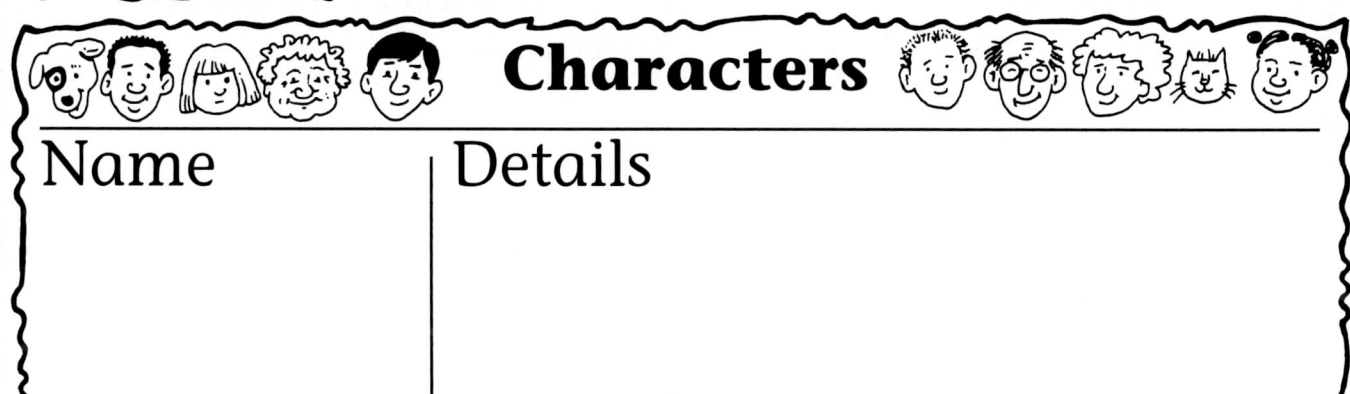

Setting

Setting 1	Setting 2	Setting 3

Characters

Name	Details

Plot

Order of events

Ending

Writing Frame for Book 4, Unit 1

Summaries

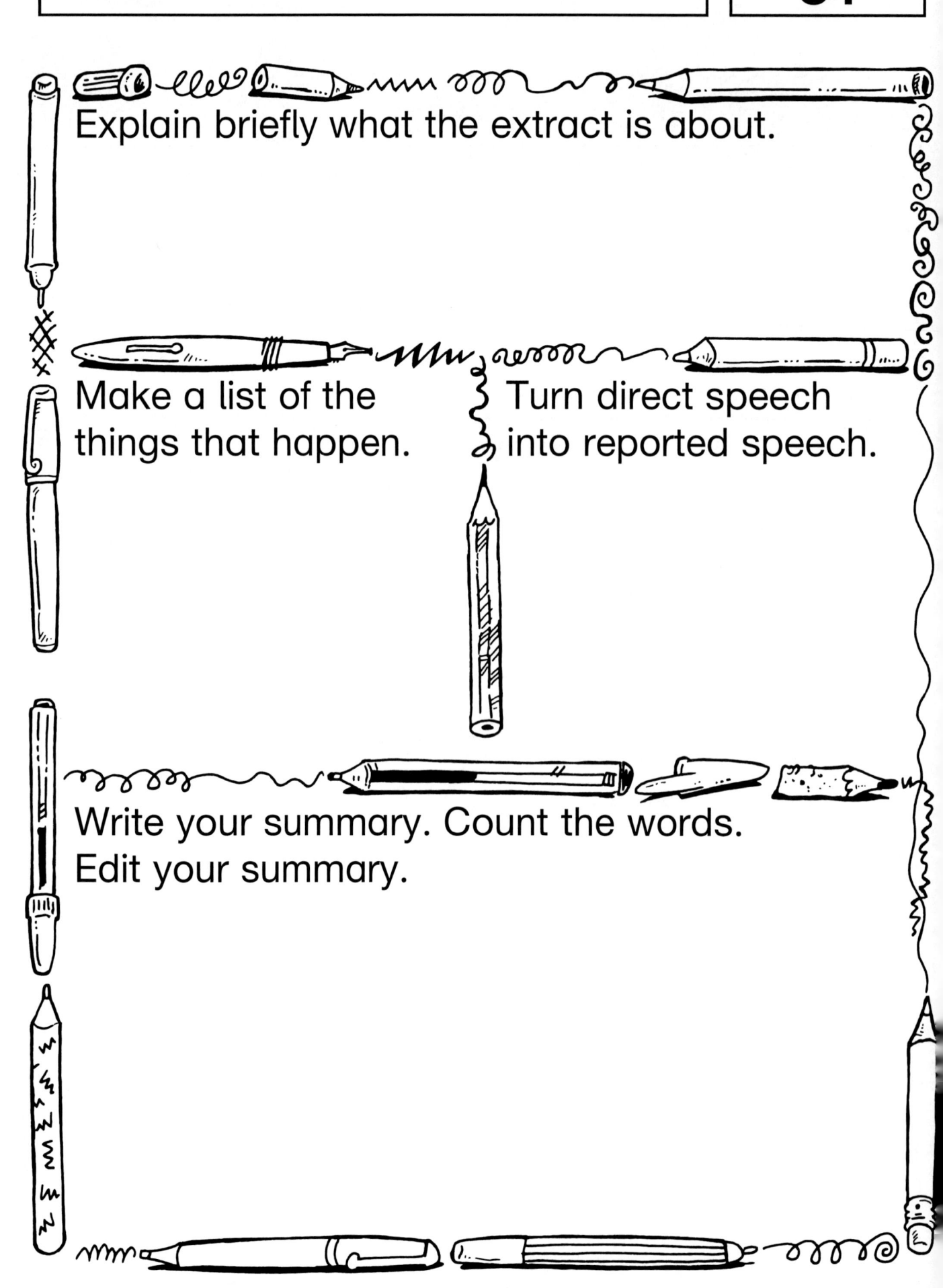

Name _____

Writing Frame
84

Explain briefly what the extract is about.

Make a list of the things that happen.

Turn direct speech into reported speech.

Write your summary. Count the words. Edit your summary.

Writing Frame for Book 4, Unit 2

Stories into playscripts

Name _____

Writing Frame 85

Story on which the playscript is based

	Can come from story	Have to make up
Scene		
Characters		
Dialogue		
Stage directions		

Brief notes on the scene

Characters' names and traits briefly

Writing Frame for Book 4, Unit 3

Focus on Writing © John Jackman and Wendy Wren, HarperCollins*Publishers* 1998
Revised edition 2004

Themes in stories and plays

Name _____

Writing Frame 86

Different versions

Book/play title

Main theme

New setting

New characters

Writing Frame for Book 4, Unit 4

Focus on Writing © John Jackman and Wendy Wren, HarperCollins*Publishers* 1998
Revised edition 2004

Personification

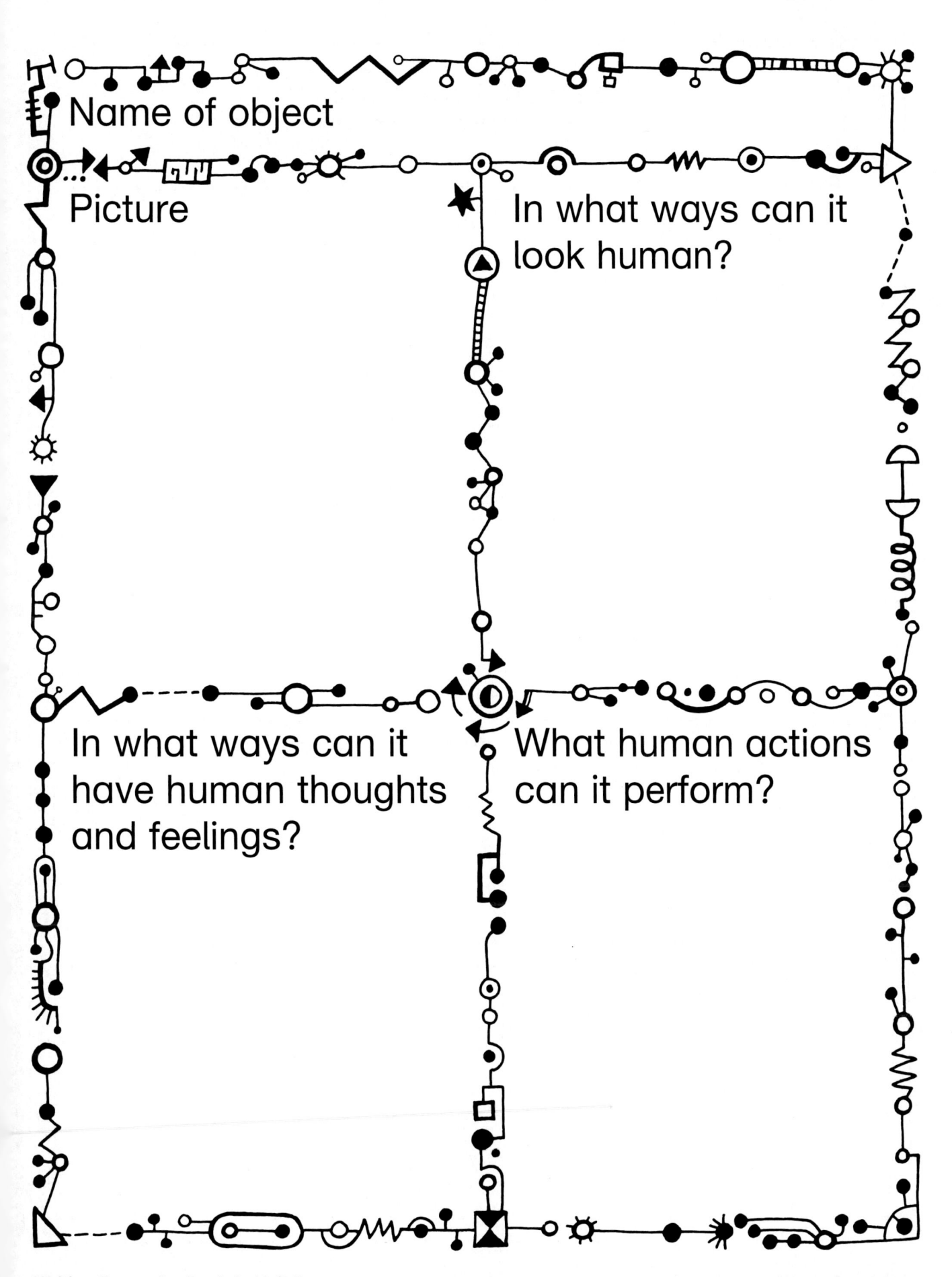

Name _____

Writing Frame 87

Name of object

Picture

In what ways can it look human?

In what ways can it have human thoughts and feelings?

What human actions can it perform?

Writing Frame for Book 4, Unit 5

Focus on Writing © John Jackman and Wendy Wren, HarperCollins*Publishers* 1998
Revised edition 2004

Biography

Name _____

Writing Frame 88

Curriculum vitae

Surname ....

Forenames ....

Date of birth ....

Address

Education

Occupations

Hobbies

Writing Frame for Book 4, Unit 6 — *Focus on Writing* © John Jackman and Wendy Wren, HarperCollins*Publishers* 1998
Revised edition 2004

Factual writing

Name _____

Writing Frame 89

➤ Experiment ◄

Aim

Equipment

Method

Results

Conclusion

Writing Frame for Book 4, Unit 7 — *Focus on Writing* © John Jackman and Wendy Wren, HarperCollins*Publishers* 1998
Revised edition 2004

Journalism

Name _____

Writing Frame 90

Headline

Sub-heading

Byline

Illustration

Front page story

Story endings

Name _____

Writing Frame 91

Story Plot

Beginning

Middle

Endings
How do you want your reader to feel?

Ending 1	Ending 2	Ending 3

Writing Frame for Book 4, Unit 9

Dreams in stories

Name _____

Writing Frame 92

Where were you in your dream?

What did it look like?

What happened in your dream?

How did you feel?

Writing Frame for Book 4, Unit 10

Focus on Writing © John Jackman and Wendy Wren, HarperCollins*Publishers* 1998
Revised edition 2004

Humorous stories

Name _____

Writing Frame 93

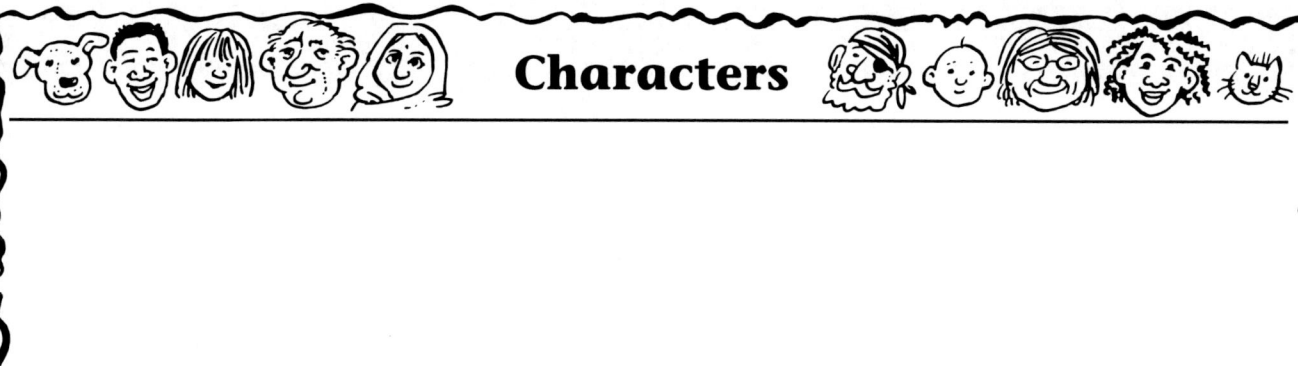

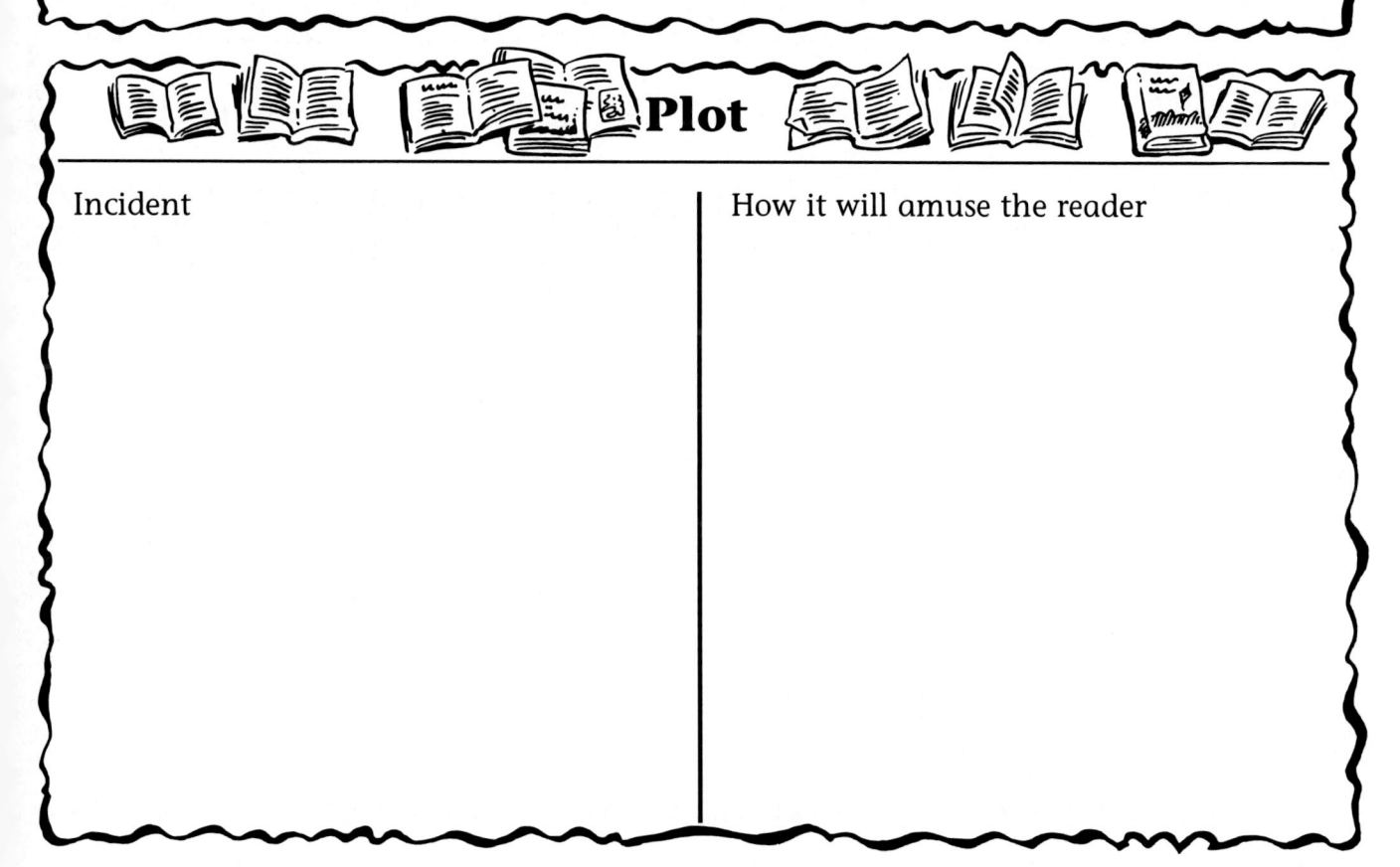

Setting

Characters

Plot

Incident	How it will amuse the reader

Writing Frame for Book 4, Unit 11 — *Focus on Writing* © John Jackman and Wendy Wren, HarperCollins*Publishers* 1998 Revised edition 2004

Making an argument

Name _____

Writing Frame 94

Topic

Are you for or against?

Facts and reasons to support your opinion

Form of non-fiction writing

letter ☐   newspaper article ☐   report ☐

Opening paragraph

Writing Frame for Book 4, Unit 12

Focus on Writing © John Jackman and Wendy Wren, HarperCollins*Publishers* 1998
Revised edition 2004

Discursive writing

Name _____

Writing Frame 95

Topic

Arguments for

Arguments against

Balancing the arguments

Conclusion

Writing Frame for Book 4, Unit 13

Filling in forms

Name _____

Writing Frame 96

What are you applying for?

Name

✉ Address and ☎ Telephone

Age ☐   Date of birth ☐

Other information required

_____

_____

_____

Signature   Date

Writing Frame for Book 4, Unit 14

Focus on Writing © John Jackman and Wendy Wren, HarperCollins*Publishers* 1998
Revised edition 2004

Poems on similar themes

Name _____

Writing Frame 97

Subject of poems		
Point of view	First person ☐	Third person ☐
	Poem 1	Poem 2
Content		
How you want your reader to feel		
Words and phrases you could use		
Number of verses		

Writing Frame for Book 4, Unit 15

Focus on Writing © John Jackman and Wendy Wren, HarperCollins*Publishers* 1998
Revised edition 2004

Writing book blurbs

Name _____

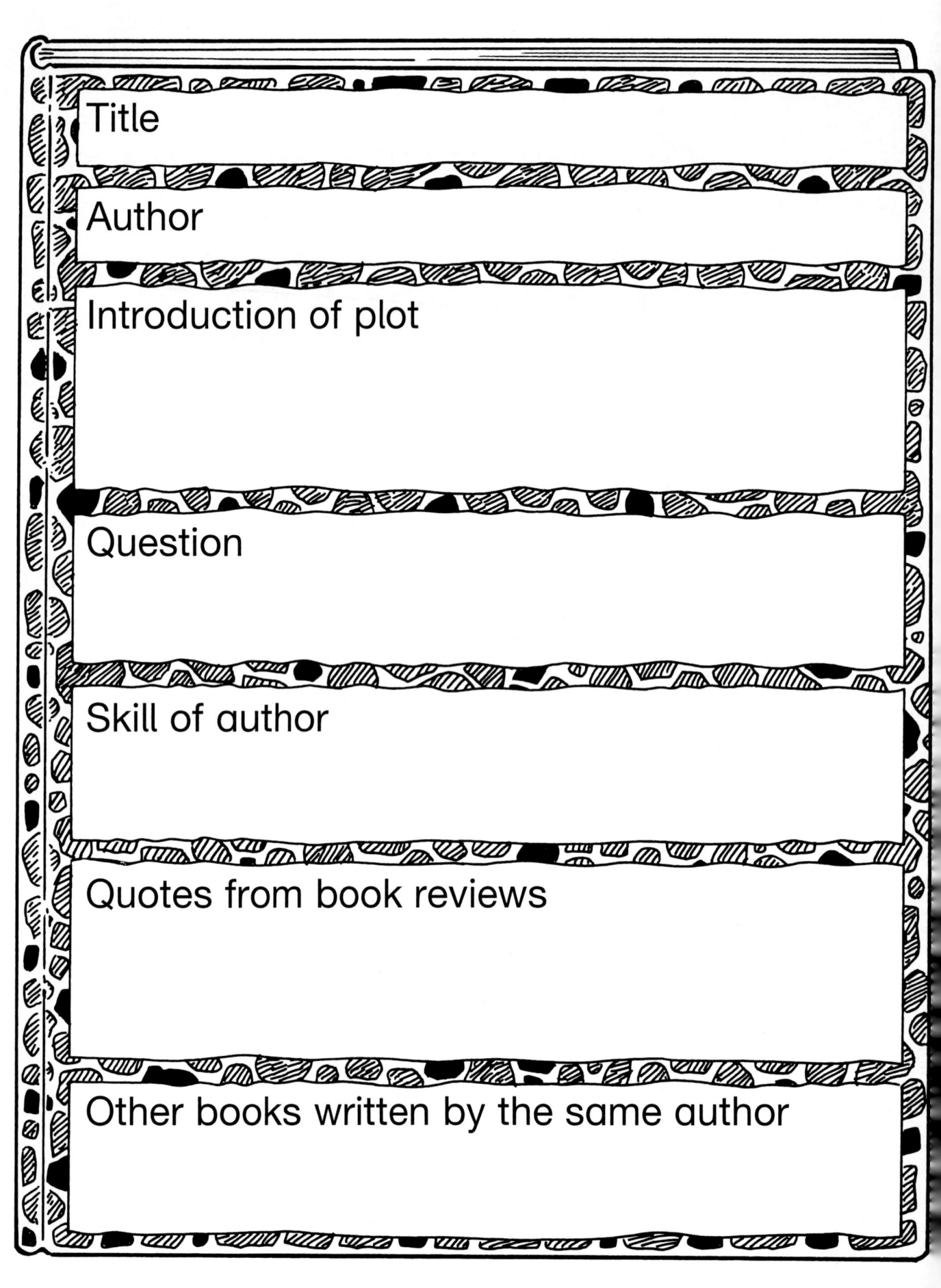

Writing Frame 98

Title

Author

Introduction of plot

Question

Skill of author

Quotes from book reviews

Other books written by the same author

A reading journal

Name _____

Writing Frame 99

Title _____

Author _____

Date I read the book _____

Fiction

Brief summary of plot

_____

Characters

_____

My opinion

Non-fiction

Sort of information

_____

How the information is presented

_____

My opinion

Writing Frame for Book 4, Unit 17

Focus on Writing © John Jackman and Wendy Wren, HarperCollins*Publishers* 1998
Revised edition 2004

Extended stories

Name _____

Writing Frame 100

Chapter

Setting	Characters	Plot

Writing Frame for Book 4, Unit 18

Focus on Writing © John Jackman and Wendy Wren, HarperCollins*Publishers* 1998
Revised edition 2004

Formal explanations

Name _____ **Writing Frame 101**

Subject

....
Introduction

....
Stage 1

....
Stage 2

....
Stage 3

....
Concluding statement

Paragraphing

Name _____ Writing Frame **102**

Main heading

Sub-heading 1
* *Key points*

Sub-heading 2
* *Key points*

Sub-heading 3
* *Key points*

Sub-heading 4
* *Key points*

Writing Frame for Book 4, Unit 20

Focus on Writing © John Jackman and Wendy Wren, HarperCollins*Publishers* 1998
Revised edition 2004

Writing for different purposes

Name _____

Writing Frame 103

Research plan

Subject: _____

Purpose of information to be collected:
_____

Main audience: _____

Useful books

Author	Title	Publisher

Notes:

Author	Title	Publisher

Notes:

Writing Frame for Book 4, Unit 21 — Focus on Writing © John Jackman and Wendy Wren, HarperCollins*Publishers* 1998
Revised edition 2004

Framing your writing

Name _____   **Writing Frame 104**

Subject:

Purpose:

Audience:

Type of frame, section 1:

Main points:

Type of frame, section 2:

Main points:

Type of frame, section 3:

Main points:

Writing Frame for Book 4, Unit 22